Extremely WEIRD

SNAKES

Text by Sarah Lovett

John Muir Publications
Santa Fe, New Mexico

Special thanks to Dale Belcher, Curator of Herpetology, Rio Grande Zoo

John Muir Publications, P.O. Box 613, Santa Fe, New Mexico 87504
© 1993 by John Muir Publications
All rights reserved. Published 1993
Printed in the United States of America

First edition. First printing July 1993.
            Second printing December 1993.
            Second TWG printing December 1993.

Library of Congress Cataloging-in-Publication Data
Lovett, Sarah, 1953-
    Snakes / text by Sarah Lovett.
        p. cm.
    Includes index.
    Summary: Describes the physical characteristics and
    behavior of twenty-two unusual snakes, including the
    puff adder, cat-eyed snake, and Brazilian rainbow boa.
      Softcover ISBN 1-56261-108-9
      Hardcover ISBN 1-56261-176-3
      1. Snakes—Juvenile literature. [1. Snakes.] I. Title.
    II. Title: Extremely weird snakes. III. Series:
    Lovett, Sarah, 1953- Extremely Weird
    QL666.06L775 1993
    597.96—dc20   93-10113
                                     CIP
                                      AC

Illustrations: Mary Sundstrom, Beth Evans
Extremely Weird Logo Art: Peter Aschwanden
Design: Sally Blakemore
Typography: Ken Wilson
Printer: Guynes Printing Company
Bindery: Prizma Industries, Inc.

Distributed to the book trade by
W. W. Norton & Co., Inc.
500 Fifth Avenue
New York, New York 10110

Distributed to the education market by
The Wright Group
19201 120th Avenue N.E.
Bothell, Washington 98011-9512

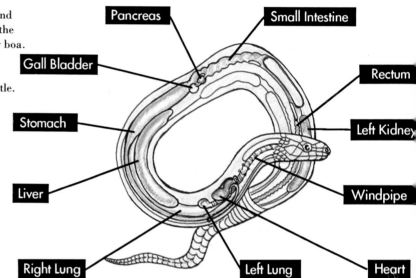

ON THE COVER: **Green Mamba (*Dendrapsis angusticeps*)**
Mambas are active, aggressive, and venomous. They are found in Africa, and they are relatives of
cobras and coral snakes. The longest mambas may grow to a length of 4.26 meters (14 feet). This
young mamba hatchling may be as much as seven times longer than its egg.

Cover photo, Green Mamba, Animals Animals © Anthony Bannister

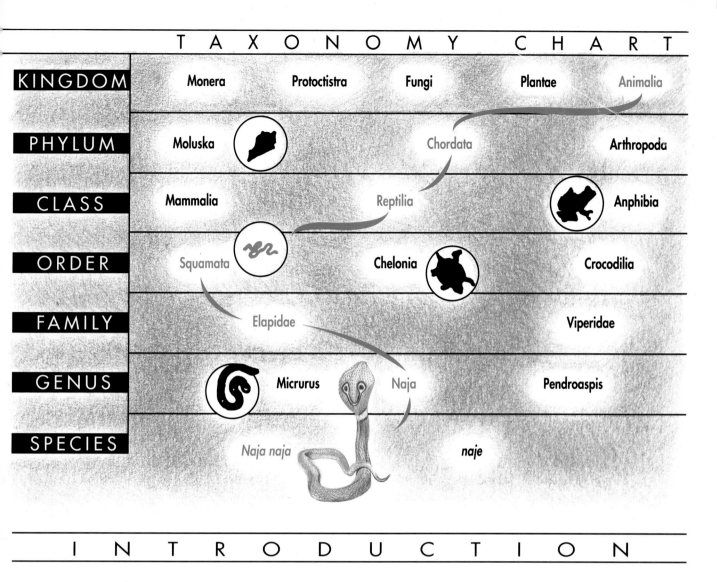

T A X O N O M Y   C H A R T

KINGDOM	Monera	Protoctistra	Fungi	Plantae	Animalia
PHYLUM	Moluska		Chordata		Arthropoda
CLASS	Mammalia		Reptilia		Anphibia
ORDER	Squamata		Chelonia		Crocodilia
FAMILY	Elapidae				Viperidae
GENUS	Micrurus		Naja		Pendroaspis
SPECIES	*Naja naja*		*naje*		

I N T R O D U C T I O N

What's so snaky about snakes? They have a long, limbless body and elongated internal organs. They also have multiple-hinge joints in their lower jaw—the better to come unhinged and fit over prey that may be larger than they are. (Snakes swallow their food whole!)

The skin of snakes is covered with scales that can be rough or smooth. Snakes and all reptiles—even aquatic species—have lungs and they breathe air. They also have backbones, which is why they're known as chordates. Many snakes lay eggs. Some snakes bear live young.

Snakes (and other reptiles) depend on their outside environment for body heat: they are ectothermic. That's why you might see a snake sunbathing on a rock. (Mammals like us, in contrast, have a constant internal body temperature.)

Some snakes are extremely poisonous. (You should *never* handle snakes in the wild because even harmless snakes may bite when they're threatened.) Out of 3,000 species worldwide, perhaps 800 species are venomous, but only about 250 species are considered dangerous to humans. Most snakes are no threat to humans at all. In fact, snakes are beneficial because they eat rodents and insects. Many snake species are endangered by pollution, over-collection, and loss of habitat (living space). All snakes need to be treated with respect and caution by humans.

To keep track of snakes and the millions of animal and plant species on earth, scientists use a universal system called taxonomy. Taxonomy begins with the five main groups of all living things, the kingdoms, and then divides those into the next group down, the phylum, then class, order, family, genus, and finally, species. Members of a species look similar, and they can reproduce with each other.

For an example of how taxonomy works, follow the highlighted lines above to see how Asiatic cobras (*Naja naja* group) are classified. In this book, the scientific name of each snake is listed next to the common name. The first word is the genus, and the second word is the species.Turn to the *glossarized index* at the back of this book if you're looking for a specific reptile, or for special information (how snakes *constrict* their prey, for instance), or if you find a word you don't understand.

The Squeeze

GREEN TREE PYTHON (*Chondropython viridis*)

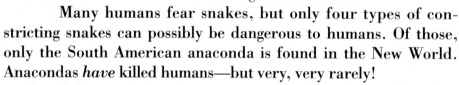

MARY SUNDSTROM

Boas and pythons are giants among snakes. They kill their prey by constriction. Usually an animal is first caught by the snake's teeth. (The green tree python from New Guinea has very big front teeth—the better to grasp startled prey on the run.) Then, almost instantly, the snake coils its body around its victim until it suffocates. Two or three extremely tight coils are usually enough to stop the prey's breathing and heart beat.

Many humans fear snakes, but only four types of constricting snakes can possibly be dangerous to humans. Of those, only the South American anaconda is found in the New World. Anacondas *have* killed humans—but very, very rarely!

A female python keeps her egg clutch warm by shivering. This uses lots of energy, and she may lose as much as half her body weight between egg-laying and hatching. It may take two or three years before she has regained enough of her energy reserves to breed again.

South American anacondas are the world's largest snakes. They have been rumored to reach lengths of 12 meters (about 40 feet), but no one is sure. On the record, reticulated pythons have measured in at lengths of nearly 10 meters (about 33 feet)!

Anacondas and reticulated pythons are both expert swimmers, and the python even swims in saltwater. It was one of the first reptiles to reach Krakatoa (by water) from neighboring Sumatra or Java after the 1888 volcanic eruption which destroyed all life on the tiny island.

BETH EVANS

Green tree pythons are the color of green leaves. They blend in perfectly with their forest surroundings.

WESTERN DIAMONDBACK RATTLESNAKE (*Crotalus atrox*)

North American rattlesnakes, South American fer-de-lances, and copperheads and moccasins (found in many parts of the world) are all known as pit vipers. Pit vipers are named for their sixth sense, an organ (or pit) that is located between each nostril and each eye. This organ can sense changes in temperature, which allows the snake to detect body heat given off by prey. With the aid of their sixth sense, pit vipers can strike on target and inject venom into their victim's body. This is especially important because pit vipers hunt mostly at night, in the dark.

After a pit viper strikes, its victim usually lives long enough to travel a distance from its predator. How does the snake know where to find its wounded prey? Two internal cavities located near the snake's snout connect to its mouth. These are filled with nerve ends (very much like the ones used for smelling) that enable the snake to trail its victim. Often, snakes with this ability also have a separate and very good sense of smell.

The western diamondback rattlesnake lives in western regions of North America. It grows to a length of more than 2 meters (about 7 feet), and it feeds mostly on rodents.

Water moccasins are pit vipers. They're also the only poisonous water snakes in the United States.

Rattlesnakes are part of Native American myth, medicine, religion, and folklore. The world-famous Hopi Indian snake dance lasts nine days. On the last day, priests actually dance with rattlesnakes. When the dance ends, the snakes are released in the four directions, and their job is to carry a positive message to the rain gods. But don't you try dancing with snakes: viper bites can be fatal.

Photo, facing page: Animals Animals © Michael Dirk

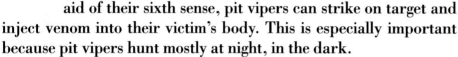

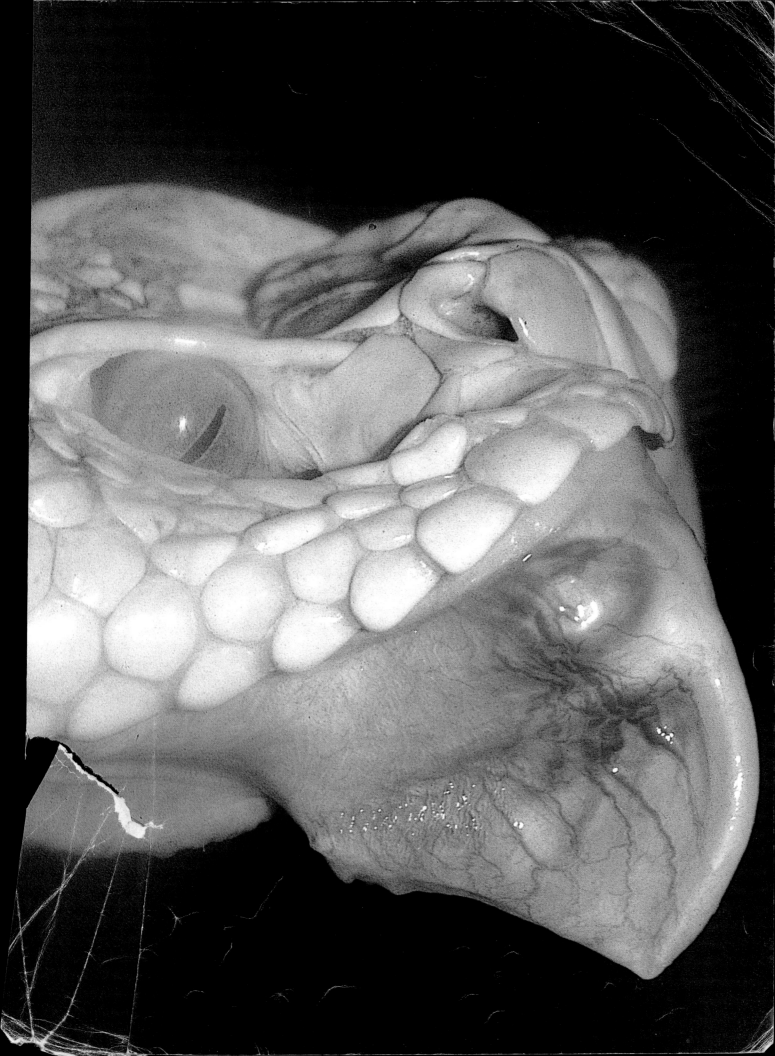

CALIFORNIA KING SNAKE
(*Lampropeltis getula californiae*)

This California king snake is an albino, so it is especially unusual. An albino is any animal (human or otherwise) who lacks pigment; for this reason, it has very white skin and pink eyes. A normal California king snake is one of North America's most colorful snakes— banded or striped, black and yellow.

All king snakes have smooth scales, and they usually grow to a length of three to four feet. Although they eat lizards, frogs, small mammals, and eggs, they also prey on other snakes—even venomous ones. Immunity to snake venom is a characteristic of snake-eating snakes from all continents.

When it hunts, the king snake strikes, wraps its body around its prey, and then kills by constriction the same way giant boas and pythons do. It usually hunts at dawn or dusk.

King snakes are oviparous, which means their young hatch out of eggs. There are usually about ten eggs per clutch (batch). Eastern, speckled, and desert king snakes are close relatives of California king snakes. They live on rocky hillsides and in meadows and woodlands in the southern United States.

Although the Age of Reptiles (which lasted about 120 million years) ended about 70 million years ago, more than 6,500 reptile species exist today, and of those, roughly 3,000 species are snakes. Snakes live almost everywhere in the world except arctic regions.

Although a warm tropical forest is almost always snake country, there are no snakes native to Hawaii.

King snakes earned their name because they prey on venomous snakes.

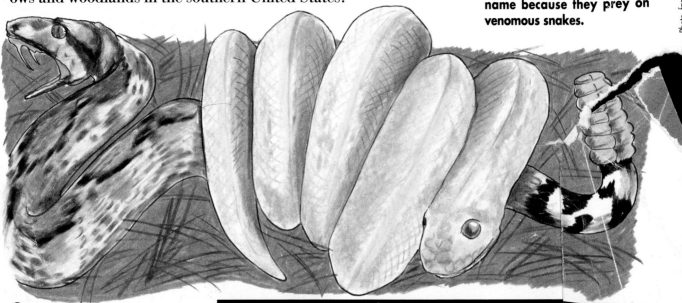

Photo, facing page, Photo Researchers, Inc., courtesy Steinhart Aquarium © Tom McHugh

BLUNT-HEADED TREE SNAKE (*Imantodes cenchoa*)

No doubt about it, blunt-headed tree snakes are weird looking: they have an extremely slim body, a big head, and big eyes. They also do weird things—such as act like an I-beam girder to bridge the gaps between branches where they hang out. Blunt-headed tree snakes will change their shape slightly and stiffen their body to reach a distant branch. Once they firmly attach to the new branch, their body relaxes again.

Blunt-headed tree snakes become active at dusk, and they hunt—for anoles, geckos, and other lizards—during the night. In daylight, they prefer to coil and rest in leaf clumps or in the leaf whorls of bromeliad plants. Several blunt-headed tree snakes may share the same resting place.

Blunt-headed tree snake habitat extends from the forests of southern Mexico to Bolivia and Paraguay. They hatch from eggs, and adults may reach a length of more than 100 centimeters (over 3 feet).

More than 250 million years ago, reptiles first crept out of the shallow seas and ventured on land. The evolutionary effort was worth it; on land, there were plenty of insects to eat and dense forests for shelter. Today, lizards, turtles, snakes, crocodilians, and the rare tuatara are the five groups of reptiles found on earth.

Blunt-headed tree snakes have fangs in the rear of their mouth. They strike their prey swiftly and accurately.

S N A K E S

PARROT SNAKE (*Leptophis* sp.)

Parrot snakes—and most other harmless or slightly venomous snakes—belong to the scientific family *Colubridae*. Members of this family range from blunt-headed burrowers to water snakes to long, slender tree dwellers.

Parrot snakes have adapted to life in small trees and shrubs in the forests of southern Mexico, Central America, and South America. They are usually blue-green (like the parrots they are named for), and they forage among the leaves for lizards and frogs, their main prey.

The parrot snake is oviparous, and there are usually four to six eggs per clutch. A newly hatched parrot snake will measure between 25 and 30 centimeters (10 and 12 inches) long, while the adult can be more than 1.20 meters (4 feet) in length.

When it is threatened, a parrot snake coils its body and opens its mouth, ready to strike!

Of all reptiles, snakes are probably the most endangered. Loss of habitat (living space) is one of the biggest threats. So is the automobile. Wherever there are roads, snakes are in danger of being run over.

S N A K E S

SOUTHERN RING-NECK SNAKE (*Diadophis punctatus*)

Do you know someone who is scared to death of snakes? Most of us do. Why? Some snakes are deadly and should be feared, but as we've already discovered, most snakes pose no real threat to humans. Why are so many of us afraid of snakes?

Snakes are long, slithery, and silent. They are also secretive, so often they are misunderstood. Snakes have also played the bad guy in myths, folktales, and cartoons. Usually, when people take the time to learn about snakes, they lose much of their fear and gain respect.

Pick up a rock or peer under a log in North America or Central America and you might find a ring-neck snake peering back at you. A ring-neck snake poses no threat to humans, but it has a way of letting you know when it is threatened by you. It hides its head under its coiled body and curls up its tail to show off a rusty or yellowish color on its underside. It may also give off a bad-smelling odor to discourage hungry predators.

These ground-dwelling snakes are named for the yellow or orange ring around their neck. They feed mostly on lizards, salamanders, young snakes, and worms. They kill their prey by constriction. Of course, they don't have to constrict worms.

Scared of snakebite? In the United States, you're more likely to die from a lightning strike (and your chances of that are slim!) than a snakebite.

Some fears—called phobias—are not based on reason. They can be hard to get over. Many people have phobias about flying in airplanes or staying in small spaces or about spiders or snakes. Specialists know how to help people overcome their phobias.

Photo, facing page, Animals Animals © Robert A. Lubeck

S N A K E S

CAT-EYED SNAKE (*Leptodeira* sp.)

Cat-eyed snakes are named for their elliptical (curved), vertical pupils that lend them a catty look. Their pupils admit or shut out light more efficiently than round pupils.

Other senses aid cat-eyed snakes when they are on the prowl. All snakes (and some lizards) have special cells—known as the Jacobson's organ—on the roof of their mouth. The Jacobson's organ helps them "smell" and "taste" with their tongue. A snake's forked tongue picks up chemical particles in the air. When the tongue is flicked around inside the mouth, the particles are transferred to the Jacobson's organ. This ability to taste and smell aids the snake as it detects enemies or as it searches for prey or a mate.

Cat-eyed snakes are both terrestrial and arboreal, which means they spend their time on the ground and in trees. They range from Arizona in the north to Argentina in the south, but most are found in northern South America.

For centuries, snakes have played important roles in literature, religion, and mythology. After all, it was a Biblical serpent who enticed Eve to sample the forbidden fruit. And Shakespeare's Cleopatra poisoned herself with the help of an asp, an Egyptian snake.

Cat-eyed snakes feed on lizards, frogs, and other small animals. The snake in this picture is dining on frog's eggs.

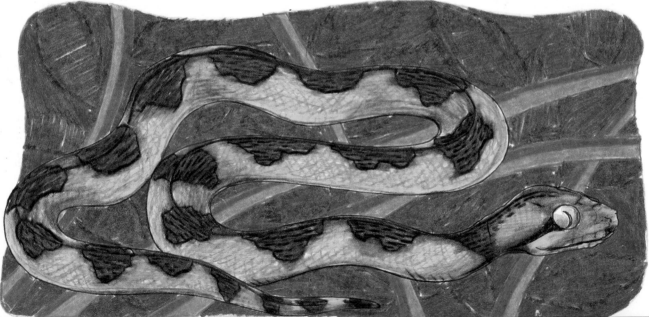

S N A K E S

RED RAT SNAKE (*Elaphe guttata*)

All snakes molt (shed their skin) from time to time, and young snakes molt more frequently. They do this because they need room to grow and also because they need to replace old, worn-out skin.

As a snake's outer skin begins to loosen from the new skin underneath, its eyes become temporarily cloudy—they're covered with skin, too!—and its eyesight dims. For this reason, a molting snake is extremely vulnerable to predators, and it will usually go into hiding until the old skin is completely shed. When a snake molts, it also becomes very touchy and aggressive. A normally harmless snake will bite if it is disturbed.

To molt, this North American red rat snake loosens the old skin around its head and lips and then crawls out of its "wrapper." Although the snake loses its appetite several days before the molt, it returns to its normal activities when its skin is entirely shed.

Rat snakes are terrestrial and arboreal. On their belly, they have a sharp plate that helps them get a grip on bark as they climb trees. They feed on birds and eggs in trees and small mammals in their burrows below ground. Rat snakes kill their prey by constriction.

All snakes lack eyelids. Instead, their eyes are covered by skin cells. Just like the skin on the rest of its body, this thin eye covering is shed when the snake molts.

Molting continues throughout a snake's lifetime. Most reptiles never stop growing, and they need new skin to help protect them from environmental wear and tear and from predators.

A snake's scales are thick segments of skin. They are mostly made of keratin, and they are a lot like your fingernails.

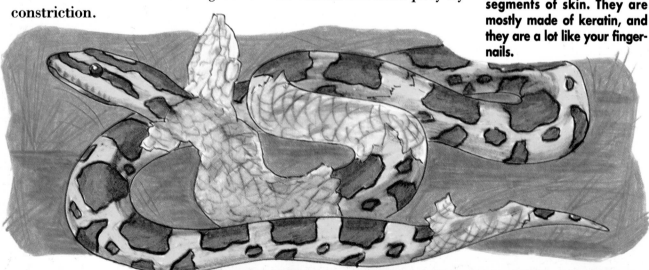

S N A K E S

Don't Get Rattled!

BLACK-TAILED RATTLESNAKE (*Crotalus molossus*)

In the deserts of the southwestern United States and Mexico, a high-pitched buzz warns passersby that the black-tailed rattlesnake is near.

A rattlesnake's rattle is a signal to larger animals to stay away! If they heed the warning, the snake avoids injury, and so does the horse, deer, cow, human, or whatever creature may be in harm's way.

The rattle consists of a series of hard, horny sections at the end of the snake's tail. Actually, each section is unshed skin, and one is added every time the snake molts.

Newly born rattlesnakes have a prebutton, a large scale at the tip of their tail. The first time young rattlesnakes molt, the prebutton is lost and section number one (the button formed underneath) appears. Several more loose sections must develop before young snakes can really rattle. It is these sections moving against each other when the tail is vibrated that produces the high-pitched sound. Most adult rattlesnakes have no more than eight rattles because those sections at the end of the tail tend to wear down or fall off with age.

Black-tailed rattlesnakes prefer rocky areas, and they are more likely than other rattlesnake species to be active during the day. They may reach a length of about 1.22 meters (4 feet), and they feed mostly on rodents.

There are 29 species of rattlesnakes, and they are all viviparous, which mean they produce live young. Rattlesnake habitats range all the way from Saskatchewan, Canada, to Argentina in South America.

Rattlesnake venom is cloudy and mostly made of proteins. Venoms have neurotoxic elements that affect the nervous system of victims.

S N A K E S

RHINOCEROUS VIPER (*Bitis nasicornis*)

In the forests of Central Africa, the colorful rhinocerous viper coils, ready to strike with its extremely large fangs. Once venom is injected into prey, the snake tracks down its dying victim and then swallows it whole. Can you imagine swallowing a chicken or a cow (or even a stalk of broccoli) whole? Of course, such a thing would be impossible for us humans, but some snakes can swallow a small deer whole. How can they get so much food into their mouth at one time? Snake jaws are specially designed for big mouthfuls. The bone that connects the lower jaw to the snake's skull works like a double-jointed hinge: the jaw drops open at the back and at the front. Also, the two bones of the lower jaw can stretch sideways because the chin muscles are very elastic.

Still hard to believe? Sharp teeth curving toward the snake's throat keep prey in place. Shifting its jaws side to side, bite by bite, the snake then "walks" its mouth over its victim.

Rhinocerous vipers—some of the most colorful true vipers—have skin that is purple and blue with green triangles. This irregular geometric pattern blends in amazingly with leaves on the forest floor. These vipers are named for large scales covering the tip of their snout, which can be raised to an erect position.

If you are bitten by a venomous snake, you should receive medical attention as soon as possible. Long ago, people believed that holding "snake stones" (made of animal bone or horn) against a wound would cure snakebites. Unfortunately, they were wrong.

True vipers are found in Europe, Asia, and Africa.

S N A K E S

Charmed

ASIATIC COBRAS (*Naja naja* group)

Cobras, coral snakes, mambas and sea snakes are members of a group of extremely dangerous venomous snakes that have venom-conducting fangs fixed at the front end of their jaw. The other group of extremely dangerous venomous snakes have much larger folding fangs that tuck backward when they are not in use.

Southeast Asia, Africa, and India are cobra country. Asiatic cobras are not aggressive. You might say they don't go looking for trouble, but if trouble comes their way, watch out! Cobra venom is so potent it can cause death in humans and other large animals; about 10 percent of cobra bites are fatal. Most cobra attacks on humans happen at night, in the dark, when people accidentally step on snakes.

To avoid trouble, cobras use a defensive, or warning, posture that warns other animals to stay away. The Asiatic cobra has very long ribs that can push out its neck skin like a hood. When the hood is fully displayed, it is much wider than the snake's body. In defensive posture, one-third of the cobra's body rises straight up while the rest is coiled.

Cobras are famous as the snake charmer's snake of choice. How do snake charmers train their snakes? They don't. Snakes can't learn tricks, but they can be handled by humans. Snake charmers cool their snakes down before a show. A cool snake is slow and passive—and easier to handle. Unfortunately, many human "charmers" do not treat their snakes in a humane way.

King cobras are famous for a very weird moan. They are also the world's largest cobra, but they usually attack humans only when they are provoked or when their nest is threatened. The female king cobra is the only cobra that builds her own nest. She makes a crook in the forepart of her body and drags leaves and sticks into a pile. Her eggs go on the bottom compartment, and then the female (and sometimes the male) stands guard on the upper compartment.

Photo: Farina naga, Animals Animals © Michael Dick

SNAKES

GREEN VINE SNAKE (*Oxybelis fulgidus*)

Some snakes play dead when threatened. They roll over, wiggle and quiver, hiss, and let their tongue loll out of their open mouth as they "die." They may remind you of actors in "B" movies.

Vine snakes spend much of their lives in trees doing nothing. At least it seems that way. Vine snakes hang motionless for hours and hours. Because their body is long and thin and bright green and their snout is slender, they resemble the green vines that surround them.

Even though a passing lizard probably won't see the snake for the vine, the vine snake will see the lizard. A green vine snake has eyes that face forward (this gives it binocular vision), and it is a good judge of distances—the better to lunge at passing prey.

The green vine snake *Oxybelis fulgidus* lives in South America, but some *Oxybelis* species are found as far north as Arizona. Other types of green vine snakes live in tropical forests in Southeast Asia.

Another Asian tree snake, the flying or gliding snake, can jump from branch to branch and glide through the air with the greatest of ease, at least for short distances.

S N A K E S

REAR-FANGED SNAKE (*Pliocerus euryzonos*)

Poisonous snakes live in many parts of the world, but they are most numerous in tropical areas. To inject venom, snakes use specially adapted teeth or fangs. Most dangerous venomous snakes are front-fanged; their enlarged fangs or teeth are located at the front of the upper jaw. In contrast, rear-fanged snakes have enlarged fangs at the back of their jaw.

The earliest venomous snakes might have been rear-fanged. Teeth located at the rear of the mouth can exert the greatest force on a victim.

The rear-fanged snake *Pliocerus euryzonos* lives in the rain forests of Costa Rica.

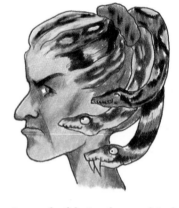

Instead of hair, the mythical Medusa sported a head full of writhing snakes. Not only would one glance at her turn viewers into stone, it was impossible for her to change her hairstyle.

Some rear-fanged snakes have adapted specially to eating snails.

SNAKES

PÉRINGUEY'S ADDER (*Bitus peringueyi*)

Péringuey's adders and their relatives are some of the deadliest snakes in Africa. Although their venom does not work as quickly as that of a cobra or a mamba, it is powerful enough to kill.

Péringuey's adders are also known as puff adders. They are so named for their ability to huff and puff—a warning to potential predators. Puff adders are called "sidewinders" because they have a unique way of traveling over sand; this form of sidewinding locomotion leaves a telltale trail. Adders lift loop after loop of their body free and clear of the surface. This form of locomotion is best for cruising across soft sand and dunes.

A puff adder has a very large head to make room for extremely large venom glands. Its body and tail are short—puff adders grow to a length of about 1 to 1.25 meters (3 to 4 feet)—and the péringuey's adder is even shorter.

Some adders would rather flee than fight, and they may vanish before your very eyes. Does that sound like magic? Some species are nifty burrowers, and they can disappear below desert sand in less than a minute.

The Péringuey's adder is a true viper, a member of the scientific family *Viperidae*. The world's smallest vipers may be less than 30 centimeters (1 foot) long, while the largest—the gaboon—may reach a length of 1.8 meters (6 feet) and a width of 15.24 centimeters (6 inches)!

The four most common methods of snake locomotion are serpentine motion, rectilinear motion, concertina motion, and sidewinding. During serpentine motion, the snake pushes its body against uneven ground. Rectilinear motion is slooowww motion; belly scales provide traction. When the snake bunches and straightens its muscles to move forward, it is using the concertina method of locomotion. You already know about sidewinding.

Photo, facing page, Animals Animals © Anthony Bannister

S N A K E S

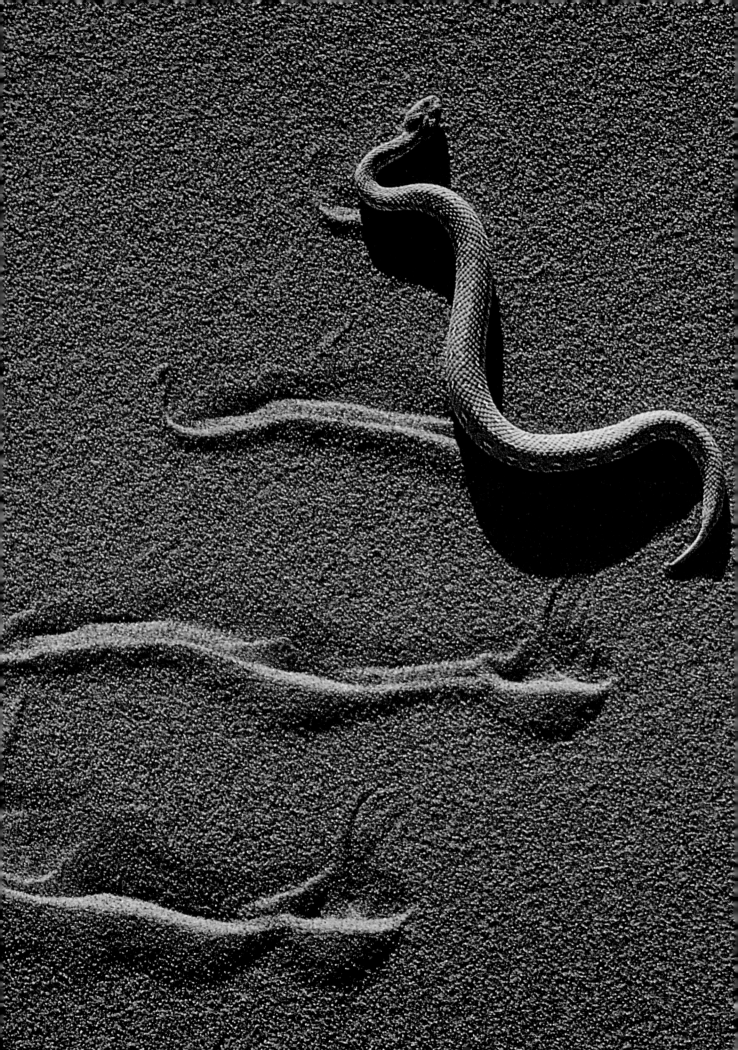

A Bevy of Boas

BRAZILIAN RAINBOW BOA (*Epicrates cenchris*)

Boas are known for their extremely colorful and iridescent skin. This rainbow coloring might seem like the last thing snakes could hide behind, but that's exactly what they do. Orange, yellow, and black patterned Brazilian rainbow boas become almost invisible when sunlight dapples the leaves in their forest habitats in South and Central America. In the right light, you can't see the snakes for the trees.

It is just as difficult to pick out one Brazilian rainbow boa from all the others when they cluster together. Adult boas sometimes form clusters during the mating season. These boas are viviparous, which means they bear live young rather than lay eggs.

Pythons and boas are deaf, but they can "feel" loud noises with their tongues. In fact, a snake's tongue is three sense organs in one: it can touch, smell, and hear.

In cooler northern climates, some garter snakes crowd or coil together in dens to stay warm during winter hibernation. Although the snakes do cool over time, heat loss is reduced.

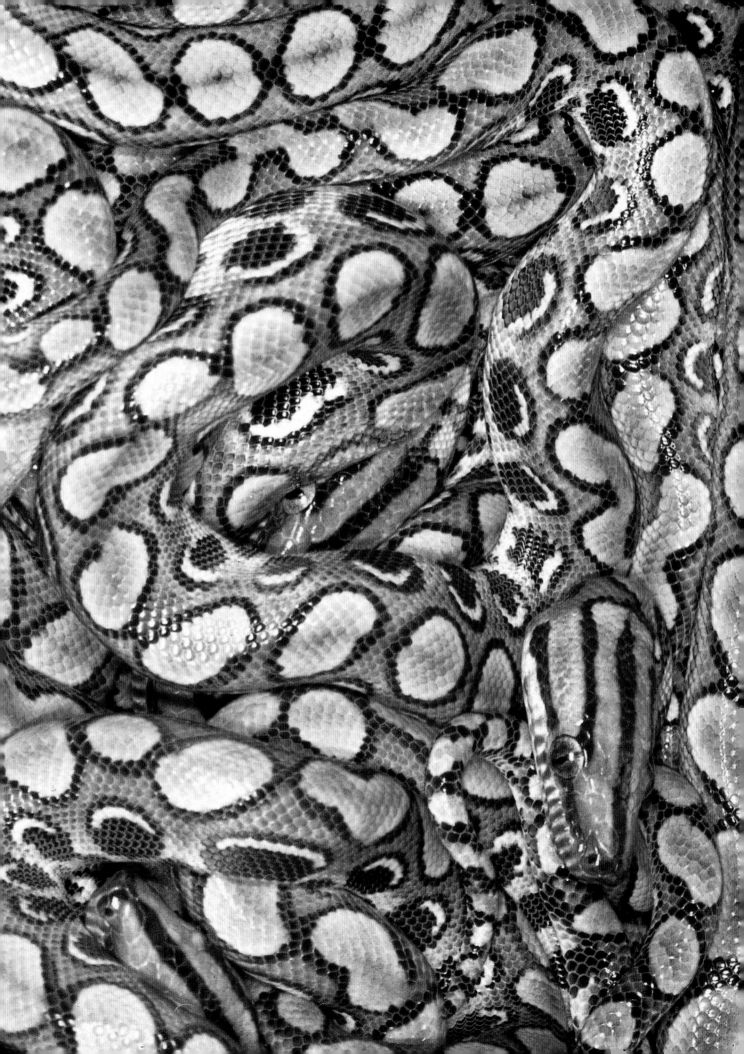

BLIND SNAKE (*Leptotyphlops dulcis*)

Blind snakes are not really blind; they *can* see dark and light. Blind snakes are able burrowers. Their round, blunt heads are made for pushing dirt. They have extremely small eyes that are hidden behind large protective scales. Blind snakes are divided into two different scientific families: *Typholopidae* and *Leptotyphlopidae*. Many live in Africa, Asia, and tropical America. A few species even live in the southwestern United States.

Depending on the species, blind snakes range in length from about 20 to 75 centimeters (8 to 30 inches). They burrow in soil and may be found under logs or stones. Blind snakes feed mostly on ants, termites, and insect larvae.

Most blind snakes lay eggs, but a few species give birth to live young.

One species of blind snake, *Typhlops braminus*, is often called the flowerpot snake because it is so small it fits easily among flowers. For this reason, the flowerpot snake has been transported to many parts of the world by accident.

Saint Patrick takes credit for snakeless Ireland. According to folklore, he banished all such reptiles from the country in order to deliver Ireland from evil.

Photo, facing page: Photo Researchers, Inc. © Larry Miller

S N A K E S

The Early Worm

EASTERN WORM SNAKE
(*Carphophis amoenus amoenus*)

Near ponds, streams, and marshes, or beneath stones and under rotting logs, you might discover the eastern worm snake feeding on slugs and (you guessed it) worms.

The eastern worm snake often hides in damp soil, and it stays deep underground in cold or dry weather. Spring is the season when you are most likely to happen upon this snake.

Eastern worm snakes have smooth and glossy skin. They are blackish-brown except on their underside, which is red or pink.

From southern New England to northern Georgia to southern Iowa, Louisiana, and Oklahoma—this is eastern worm snake territory.

Some burrowing snakes have a large scaled shield on their tail. This may be used to block the entrance of their burrow once they are safely inside.

At some point in their evolution, snakes probably went underground. As burrowers, they did not need keen eyesight or acute hearing. Instead, they probably depended on the ability to detect vibrations and heat variations to find prey and avoid predators.

Photo, facing page, Photo Researchers, Inc. © Jeff Lepore

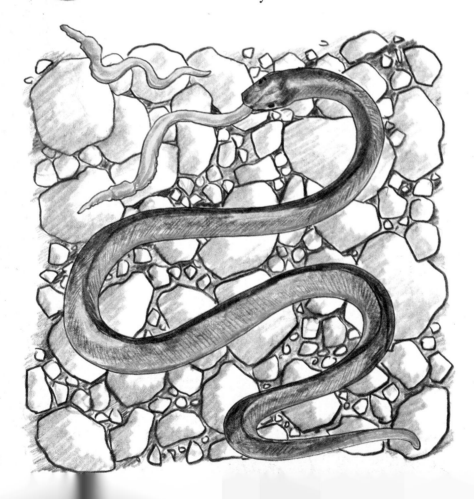

MEXICAN CANTIL (*Agkistrodon bilineatus*)

Mexican cantils are pit vipers—just like rattlesnakes and fer-de-lances—and they use their special pit organ to locate and accurately strike and inject venom into their prey. But Mexican cantils are different from many of their relatives because they sometimes do much of their hunting near or in water.

The Mexican cantil feeds on fish, frogs, birds, and small animals along lakeshores and stream banks in Mexico and farther south. It is also known as the Mexican moccasin, and it is a relative of the North American water moccasin.

In skin pattern, a young cantil resembles yet another type of pit viper, the copperhead, with its bright yellow bands and yellow-tipped tail. The tail comes in very handy; when it is slowly wiggled, it acts as a lure for curious prey.

Mexican cantils retain their bold coloring when they are adults, but they develop different patterns. They also sport a blood-red forked tongue. They may reach a length of 1.5 meters (5 feet), and their body is thick.

Another pit viper, the eyelash viper, is named for the horny scales—a scaly eyelash—above its eyes. Because they are often found in tropical fruit trees, especially banana trees, eyelash pit vipers have accidentally traveled to many parts of the world on banana boats.

AFRICAN EGG-EATING SNAKE (*Dasypeltis scabra*)

You've probably eaten an egg for breakfast, but have you swallowed the shell, too? African egg-eating snakes are egg specialists. They eat only birds' eggs that are hard-shelled. Their mouth and neck are amazingly expandable and flexible. In fact, they may swallow an egg that is twice as wide as their body! The bones in their neck and back are long and sharp and spiny and act as a saw. As the snake swallows, the egg passes though the throat and is pushed up against the neck bones; the shell is cracked and crushed.

Using muscle power, the snake squeezes the contents of the egg all the way to its stomach. The snake curves its body to force the shell and membrane back to the mouth, where they are spit out or regurgitated.

Egg-eating snakes can devour as many eggs as they find at one time. It may take only minutes or as long as an hour to eat an egg.

Many snakes can eat the soft-shelled eggs laid by lizards and some snakes, but devouring hard-shelled eggs is the job of only a few snakes.

Snakes usually lay eggs with leathery, flexible shells. A hatchling snake uses its special egg tooth to slit a hole in the shell so it can slither out.

S N A K E S

SOUTHERN BANDED WATER SNAKE (*Nerodia fasciata pictiventris*)

Swamps, marshes, and dark slow streams of Florida, South Carolina, and Alabama are favorite places for southern banded water snakes to cruise. They are active during the day, but they are often seen basking on branches overhanging water. When disturbed, they drop instantly into the water for a quick getaway.

The southern banded water snake feeds mostly on small fish such as minnows. This is a large, heavy-bodied snake, and adults may reach a length of 1.8 meters (6 feet). Although the newly born young are only about 20 centimeters (8 inches) long, they make up for their size in number; there may be 100 or more young per birth!

What's in a common name? Cotton-mouthed snakes are named for the cottony color of their open mouth. Southern banded water snakes are named for their markings. Milk snakes are so named because some folks used to believe they actually "milked" cows.

Southern banded water snakes can be found in Florida's Everglades. Among the other animals found in this amazing area are alligators, rare birds, and plants that grow nowhere else.

Photo, facing page, Animals Animals © Joe McDonald

S N A K E S

SEA SNAKE (Family: *Hydrophidae*)

Sea snakes—relatives of cobras and coral snakes—are among the most venemous of all snakes. They live mostly in tropical coastal waters of Asia and Australia; they are never found in the Atlantic Ocean. Some species of sea snakes produce live young at sea, while other species come ashore long enough to lay their eggs. All are adapted for life in the ocean.

A sea snake can stay underwater for as long as five hours at a time. In order to swim quickly, it has a flattened, oar-like tail. It is also equipped with valvelike nostrils that control the flow of seawater. (After all, it doesn't have fingers to plug its nose.) The sea snake has a slender head—the better to squeeze into tight spaces to search for eels, its main prey.

There are about species of sea s species pictured h Australia's Coral Se

Some sea snakes reach a length of 2.4 meters (8 feet) or more!

S N A K E S

This glossarized index will help you find specific information about snakes. It will also help you understand the meaning of some of the words used in this book.

Watch for the arrival of these new series at your local bookstore. Or order direct by calling **1-800-888-7504** and receive our **free** young readers catalog.

IZARRE & BEAUTIFUL SERIES

A spirited and fun investigation of the mysteries of the five senses in the animal kingdom.

ach title is 8½" x 11", 48 pages, $14.95 hardcover, with color hotographs and illustrations throughout.

zarre & Beautiful Ears
zarre & Beautiful Eyes
zarre & Beautiful Feelers
zarre & Beautiful Noses
zarre & Beautiful Tongues

RAINBOW WARRIOR ARTISTS SERIES

W hat is a Rainbow Warrior Artist? It is a person who strives to live in harmony with the Earth and all living creatures, and who tries to better the world while living his or her life in a creative way.

Each title is written by Reavis Moore with a foreword by LeVar Burton, and is 8½" x 11", 48 pages, $14.95 hardcover, with color photographs and illustrations.

Native Artists of Africa (available 1/94)
Native Artists of North America

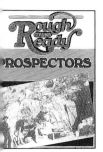

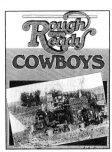

OUGH AND READY SERIES

earn about the men and women who settled the American frontier. Explore the myths and legends about these coura-geous individuals and learn about the environmental, ltural, and economic legacies they left to us.

ach title is written by A. S. Gintzler and is 48 pages, 8½" x 11", 2.95 hardcover, with two-color illustrations and duotone chival photographs.

ugh and Ready Cowboys (available 4/94)
ugh and Ready Homesteaders (available 4/94)
ugh and Ready Prospectors (available 4/94)

AMERICAN ORIGINS SERIES

M any of us are the third and fourth generation of our families to live in America. Learn what our great-great grandparents experienced when they arrived here and how much of our lives are still intertwined with theirs.

Each title is 48 pages, 8½" x 11", $12.95 hardcover, with two-color illustrations and duotone archival photographs.

Tracing Our German Roots, Leda Silver
Tracing Our Irish Roots, Sharon Moscinski
Tracing Our Italian Roots, Kathleen Lee
Tracing Our Jewish Roots, Miriam Sagan

RDERING INFORMATION
ase check your local bookstore for our books, or call 1-800-888-7504 to order direct from us. All orders are shipped via UPS; see chart to calculate your shipping charge for U.S. destinations. P.O. Boxes please; we must have a street address to ensure delivery. If the book you request is not available, we will hold your check until we can ship it. Foreign orders will be shipped sur-e rate unless otherwise requested; please enclose $3.00 for the first item and $1.00 for each additional item.

THODS OF PAYMENT
eck, money order, American Express, MasterCard, or Visa. We cannot be responsible for cash sent through the mail. For credit card orders, include your card number, expiration date, and r signature, or call (800) 888-7504. American Express card orders can be shipped only to billing address of cardholder. Sorry, no C.O.D.'s. Residents of sunny New Mexico, add 6.125% tax otal.

dress all orders and inquiries to:
n Muir Publications
. Box 613
nta Fe, NM 87504
5) 982-4078
0) 888-7504

For U.S. Orders Totaling	Add
Up to $15.00	$4.25
$15.01 to $45.00	$5.25
$45.01 to $75.00	$6.25
$75.01 or more	$7.25

EXTREMELY WEIRD SERIES

All of the titles are written by Sarah Lovett, 8¹/₂" x 11", 48 pages, $9.95 paperbacks, with color photographs and illustrations.

Extremely Weird Bats
Extremely Weird Birds
Extremely Weird Endangered Species
Extremely Weird Fishes
Extremely Weird Frogs
Extremely Weird Insects
Extremely Weird Mammals
Extremely Weird Micro Monsters
Extremely Weird Primates
Extremely Weird Reptiles
Extremely Weird Sea Creatures
Extremely Weird Snakes
Extremely Weird Spiders

X-RAY VISION SERIES

Each title in the series is 8¹/₂" x 11", 48 pages, $9.95 paperback, with color photographs and illustrations and written by Ron Schultz.

Looking Inside the Brain
Looking Inside Cartoon Animation
Looking Inside Caves and Caverns
Looking Inside Sports Aerodynamics
Looking Inside Sunken Treasure
Looking Inside Telescopes and the Night Sky

THE KIDDING AROUND TRAVEL GUIDES

All of the titles listed below are 64 pages and $9.95 paperbacks, except for *Kidding Around the National Parks* and *Kidding Around Spain*, which are 108 pages and $12.95 paperbacks.

Kidding Around Atlanta
Kidding Around Boston, 2nd ed.
Kidding Around Chicago, 2nd ed.
Kidding Around the Hawaiian Islands
Kidding Around London
Kidding Around Los Angeles
Kidding Around the National Parks
 of the Southwest
Kidding Around New York City, 2nd ed.
Kidding Around Paris
Kidding Around Philadelphia
Kidding Around San Diego
Kidding Around San Francisco
Kidding Around Santa Fe
Kidding Around Seattle
Kidding Around Spain
Kidding Around Washington, D.C., 2nd ed.

MASTERS OF MOTION SERIES

Each title in the series is 10¹/₄" x 9", 48 pages, $9.95 paperback, with color photographs and illustrations.

How to Drive an Indy Race Car
 David Rubel
How to Fly a 747
 Tim Paulson
How to Fly the Space Shuttle
 Russell Shorto

THE KIDS EXPLORE SERIES

Each title is written by kids for kids the Westridge Young Writers Workshop, 7" x 9", with photograp and illustrations by the kids.

Kids Explore America's Hispanic Heritage
112 pages, $7.95 paper
Kids Explore America's African-American Heritage
128 pages, $8.95 paper
Kids Explore the Gifts of Children with Special Needs
112 pages, $8.95 paper (available 2/94)
Kids Explore America's Japanese Heritage
112 pages, $8.95 paper (available 4/94)

ENVIRONMENTAL TITLES

Habitats: Where the Wild Things Live
Randi Hacker and Jackie Kaufman
8¹/₂" x 11", 48 pages, color illustrations, $9.95 paper

The Indian Way: Learning to Communicate with Mother Earth
Gary McLain
7" x 9", 114 pages, illustrations, $9.95 pap

Rads, Ergs, and Cheeseburgers: The Kids' Guide to Energy and the Environment
Bill Yanda
7" x 9", 108 pages, two-color illustrations, $13.95 paper

The Kids' Environment Book: What's Awry and Why
Anne Pedersen
7" x 9", 192 pages, two-color illustrations, $13.95 paper